FAIR TRADE & GLOBAL ECONOMY

by

Charlie Ogden

Crabtree Publishing Company
www.crabtreebooks.com
1-800-387-7650

Published in Canada
Crabtree Publishing
616 Welland Avenue
St. Catharines, ON
L2M 5V6

Published in the United States
Crabtree Publishing
PMB 59051
350 Fifth Ave, 59th Floor
New York, NY 10118

Published by Crabtree Publishing Company in 2018

First Published by Book Life in 2018
Copyright © 2018 Book Life

Author: Charlie Ogden

Editors: Kirsty Holmes, Janine Deschenes

Design: Danielle Jones

Proofreader: Petrice Custance

Production coordinator and
prepress technician (interior): Margaret Amy Salter

Prepress technician (covers): Ken Wright

Print coordinator: Margaret Amy Salter

Photographs
Abbreviations: l–left, r–right, b–bottom, t–top, c–centre, m–middle.

Front Cover t – Maximum Exposure PR. Front Cover b – Matej Kastelic. 2 – AlesiaKan. 4 – welcomia. 5 – Jess Kraft. 6 – tcly. 7 – Protasov AN. 8 – Chatrawee Wiratgasem. 9 – Alexander Mazurkevich. 10 – captainblueberry. 11t – Sarine Arslanian, 11b – Frontpage. 12 – Henry Tran. 13 – Phuong D. Nguyen. 14 – visa netpakdee. 15 – nathapol HPS. 16 – Dmitry Tkachenko Photo. 17 – GagliardiImages. 18 – I, SteveRwanda [GFDL (http://www.gnu.org/copyleft/fdl.html), CC–BY–SA–3.0 (http://creativecommons.org/licenses/by-sa/3.0/) or CC BY–SA 2.5–2.0–1.0 (http://creativecommons.org/licenses/by–sa/2.5–2.0–1.0)], via Wikimedia Commons. 19 – Rene Holtslag. 21cl – melis, 21c – Frame China, 21cr – Rafal Cichawa. 22l – chrisdorney, 22r – Thinglass. 23cl – By Source (WP:NFCC#4), Fair use, https://en.wikipedia.org/w/index.php?curid=20662699, 23c – TRphotos. 24 – John Wollwerth. 25 – Michael C. Gray. 26 –Arina P Habich. 27 – Andy Dean Photography. 28 – Iakov Filimonov. 29 – wavebreakmedia – Brayden Howie. 30 – takoburito.
Images are courtesy of Shutterstock.com, unless stated otherwise. With thanks to Getty Images, Thinkstock Photo and iStockphoto.

Printed in the USA/012018/BG20171102

Library and Archives Canada Cataloguing in Publication

Ogden, Charlie, author
    Fair trade and global economy / Charlie Ogden.

(Our values)
Includes index.
Issued in print and electronic formats.
ISBN 978-0-7787-4732-1 (hardcover).--
ISBN 978-0-7787-4747-5 (softcover).--
ISBN 978-1-4271-2085-4 (HTML)

    1. International trade--Moral and ethical aspects--Juvenile literature. 2. International trade--Juvenile literature. 3. Globalization--Moral and ethical aspects--Juvenile literature. 4. Globalization--Juvenile literature. 5. Social responsibility of business--Juvenile literature. 6. Work environment--Juvenile literature. I. Title.

HF1379.O34 2018   j382   C2017-906927-6
                                       C2017-906928-4

Library of Congress Cataloging-in-Publication Data

CIP available at the Library of Congress

CONTENTS

Page 4   What Is an Economy?

Page 6   Why Is There a Global Economy?

Page 8   Case Study: The Global Economic Crisis

Page 10   Effects of the Global Economy

Page 12   What Is Fair Trade?

Page 14   Fair Trade and the Global Economy

Page 18   Economies around the World

Page 22   Fair Trade and the Global Economy Today

Page 24   Fair Trade

Page 28   Get Involved!

Page 30   Activity

Page 31   Glossary

Page 32   Index

Words that look like **this** can be can be found in the glossary on page 31.

WHAT IS AN ECONOMY?

The word "economy" refers to the ways that a country or region makes and spends money. A country's economy is made up of many parts. It includes the **goods** and **services** that the people in the country use, and the amount of money they spend on them. It also includes the goods and services that people produce, and the amount of money they make from selling them. A country's economy can also refer to the **resources** it has.

THE TYPE OF MONEY USED IN A COUNTRY IS CALLED ITS CURRENCY. CURRENCY CAN DIFFER FROM COUNTRY TO COUNTRY.

Euro

American dollar

Japanese yen

British pound

Economies are often described as being strong or weak. In countries with weak economies, **citizens** have less money to spend. Fewer goods and services are bought and sold. Countries with strong economies have businesses that make a lot of money. Their citizens are able to spend a lot on goods and services. Most of the time, these countrie also have good schools, roads, and other services, because their **governments** have th money needed to spend on them. However, a country's economy can go from strong to weak very quickly. When this happens, it usually makes life difficult for its citizens.

ECONOMIES AND TRADING

Trading is the buying and selling, or exchanging of goods, services, and resources. Trade makes up a big part of economies around the world. Domestic trade happens within one country. People also sell different goods and services to people in other countries. Governments in countries sell goods, services, and resources to other governments. This is called international trading. Often, international trade happens when some countries have products and resources that others do not. For example, most of the coffee in the United States is imported, or brought in, from countries in South America and Asia. This is because coffee beans, which are used to make coffee, cannot be grown in most places in the United States. To get coffee, **organizations** or businesses have to buy coffee beans from people and businesses in countries where they can grow.

This hillside in Colombia, South America, is covered in coffee plants.

GOODS AND SERVICES BOUGHT FROM OTHER COUNTRIES ARE CALLED IMPORTS. GOODS AND SERVICES SOLD TO OTHER COUNTRIES ARE CALLED EXPORTS.

THE GLOBAL ECONOMY

International trade means that different countries and their economies are linked together. Many people refer to the international buying and selling of goods and services as the global economy.

The term is one way of looking at the complicated relationships between the economies of different countries. It is also used to talk about how one country's economy can affect another country's economy.

WHY IS THERE A GLOBAL ECONOMY?

The idea of a global economy is a fairly recent one. It is only in the last few decades that people have been studying and talking about an economy that connects all of the countries on Earth. Why is this the case?

THE STEEL CONTAINERS USED ON CONTAINER SHIPS ARE ALL EXACTLY THE SAME SIZE. ALL THE SHIPS, TRAINS, AND TRUCKS IN THE WORLD CARRY THIS SIZE OF CONTAINER. THIS MAKES IT EASY TO TRANSPORT GOODS TO ALMOST ANYWHERE.

In the last 100 years, international trade has exploded because of the advancement of technology. Today, we have container ships that can **transport** huge amounts of goods between different **ports**. Huge airplanes and trucks can also take goods across air and land. Telephones, computers, and the Internet also allow people from different parts of the world to work together, and to sell goods and services online. New technology has made global trade possible on a much larger scale, creating what we now know as the global economy.

New technology has also made it much cheaper to transport goods. To make or save the most money possible, people and organizations want to buy the least expensive goods and resources they can find. For example, a company that builds furniture might be able to buy wood from another country and ship it to their factory for a cheaper price than buying local wood. This is important, as it has allowed people to buy the cheapest goods and resources possible, and encouraged them to buy from other countries.

Canada exports more wood, or timber, than any other country in the world.

WITHOUT MODERN COMPUTER TECHNOLOGY, IT WOULD BE DIFFICULT FOR ORGANIZATIONS TO EMPLOY, OR HIRE, PEOPLE IN OTHER COUNTRIES.

It is not only goods that can be cheaper in other countries. Many businesses also hire people in other countries, because they can sometimes pay them less money than people within their country.

However, this can sometimes cause the **exploitation** of workers. In these cases, workers in other countries are not paid enough for their work.

CASE STUDY:
THE GLOBAL ECONOMIC CRISIS

The Global Economic Crisis of 2008 shows how the economies of different countries are connected as one big global economy. It also shows that the global economy can have problems. In the 1990's, banks and other moneylending organizations in the United States were letting people borrow a lot of money to buy houses. People then paid the money back a little bit at a time. This is called a mortgage loan. Since the economy was strong at that time, people had enough money to pay back their loans.

WHEN YOU PAY BACK A LOAN, YOU USUALLY HAVE TO PAY BACK MORE MONEY THAN YOU BORROWED, THROUGH SOMETHING CALLED **INTEREST**. THIS IS HOW THE ORGANIZATIONS THAT GIVE OUT LOANS MAKE MONEY.

Loans were given to many people, including those who had little savings to pay the loans back. With more people buying houses, house prices went up. To meet the demand, more houses were built. Eventually, too many houses were built. There were many more houses than what people could buy. This caused the price of houses in the United States to fall. Now, people still had loans on houses they bought at high prices, but the houses weren't worth as much money anymore.

When the economy started to weaken, people couldn't sell the houses or pay back the loans. Banks and other lenders lost a lot of money. This meant that the United States economy lost a lot of money, too. People who could not pay their loans lost their homes, and did not have the money to get back on their feet. Many other things were affected too, not just homes. When this happens to an economy, and people and businesses have less money than before, it is called an economic crash.

When people could not pay back their loans, the banks and organizations foreclosed, or took ownership of, their houses. But since the houses weren't worth as much money, the banks and organizations lost money.

When the United States's economy crashed, it caused problems for the people living there, but it also caused a global problem. The United States stopped buying as many goods and services from other countries around the world. This hurt the economies of other countries, and some of them also crashed. This caused the Global Economic Crisis, from which many countries are still recovering. The crisis shows how the economies of countries around the world are interconnected, and how they depend on each other to keep the global economy healthy.

EFFECTS OF THE GLOBAL ECONOMY

Countries are sometimes classified, or sorted, as **more economically developed countries** (MEDCs) or **less economically developed countries** (LEDCs). How economically developed a country is can be based on the **standard of living** in that country, and how much money people make there. In the global economy, it is more common for MEDCs, such as the US and Germany, to import goods and services from LEDCs, such as Vietnam and Costa Rica. This is because people and organizations in MEDCs have the money to import the things they need, such as food and fuel. Often, people and organizations in LEDCs cannot afford to import these things.

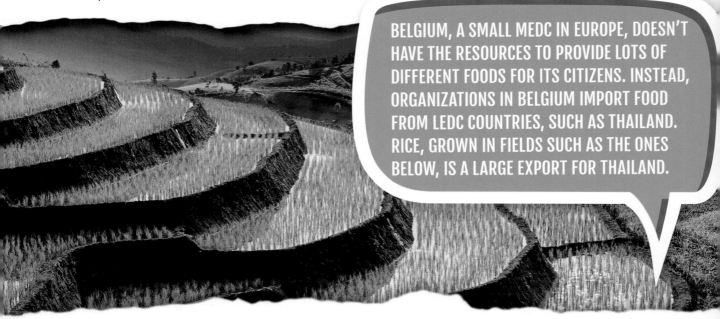

BELGIUM, A SMALL MEDC IN EUROPE, DOESN'T HAVE THE RESOURCES TO PROVIDE LOTS OF DIFFERENT FOODS FOR ITS CITIZENS. INSTEAD, ORGANIZATIONS IN BELGIUM IMPORT FOOD FROM LEDC COUNTRIES, SUCH AS THAILAND. RICE, GROWN IN FIELDS SUCH AS THE ONES BELOW, IS A LARGE EXPORT FOR THAILAND.

The global economy has had a huge impact on the world. One impact is the types of jobs that are common in different countries. People often work in jobs that are in demand in the global economy. For example, many LEDCs export crops to other countries where those crops cannot be grown. Because of this, those countries often have a larger amount of citizens working in **agriculture**. In Thailand, 40 percent of people work in agriculture-related jobs. In other countries where there are **natural resources**, such as oil, people work in jobs that extract those resources and transport them to different places.

The global economy has been shaped by the drive of people and organizations to make money. Organizations in MEDCs buy goods from other countries because they are cheap and they can sell the goods for more money. People in LEDCs can make money by selling their goods to other countries or working for businesses that have set up factories in their countries.

However, the desire to make money has sometimes led to people being exploited. Some organizations save money by paying workers very little. Often, these workers are forced to work very long days to support themselves and their families. The working **conditions** in some factories in LEDCs are very poor, and sometimes dangerous, because the organizations running them do not spend money to keep them safe. A "sweatshop" is a word used to describe a factory, usually in a LEDC, where people work very long hours in very poor conditions. Despite efforts to end sweatshop **labor**, it is still common today. The battle for workers' rights around the world is ongoing.

People in LEDCs who work in agriculture are often only paid a small amount of money for the food they produce. In many cases, this food goes on to be sold for much more money in MEDCs. Foods such as fruit, chocolate, and coffee can be some of the most expensive items in the grocery store. However, the farmers in Africa, Asia, and South America who grow the plants to produce these foods often only get a tiny portion of the money made from selling them.

This is a banana plantation in India. A plantation is a large farm where crops, or plants grown for food, are grown in order to be sold to make money.

WHAT IS FAIR TRADE?

Fair trade is the idea that global trading should be fair and **equitable**. This would mean that goods and services are bought and sold at fair prices, and that workers are not exploited. Many MEDCs have laws to make sure that people in their country trade goods and services in a fair and equal way. However, there are few international trading laws to protect people in LEDCs. Fair trade is the idea that rules should be put in place to protect citizens all around the world.

Fair trade is often concerned with the buying and selling of goods such as coffee beans, fruit, cocoa, cotton, wine, sugar, flowers, and gold. These goods are usually exported from LEDCs to wealthy MEDCs, and the people who produce them are often not treated equally or paid fairly.

LAWS ARE RULES MADE BY GOVERNMENTS THAT MUST BE FOLLOWED BY EVERYONE IN A COUNTRY. INTERNATIONAL LAWS ARE RULES THAT EVERYONE IN THE WORLD MUST FOLLOW.

Fair trade means that a fair portion of the money made from selling goods, such as bananas, should be given to the person who produced it. Paying workers fair **wages** for their goods and services helps them to grow their businesses and improve their local economies. It also allows them to support themselves and their families. For example, paying a banana farmer fair wages for their food might mean that the farmer can expand to grow more bananas, to be shipped all over the world.

Supporters of fair trade also believe in using **sustainable** farming methods. These are ways of farming that do not negatively affect the environment. Sustainable farming takes care of the land being farmed so that it can be reused. Non-sustainable farming methods are often cheaper and quicker, but they harm the environment. For example, **clear-cutting** is one way that land is cleared quickly to make room for farming. However, this is non-sustainable as the trees being cut down are not replaced. Fair trade supporters believe that farming should be sustainable even if it is more expensive or takes longer.

FAIR TRADE AND THE
GLOBAL ECONOMY

Supporters of fair trade believe that by paying farmers a fair amount for their work, they will be able to use sustainable farming methods more often, which will make Earth's environment healthier. Sustainable farming methods make sure that land is not overused, so that it can continue to produce crops in the future. Sustainable farming methods also help protect the environment and reduce the impact that farming has on animals and plants.

Many non-sustainable methods are cheap, but can be dangerous in the long-term. For example, chemicals called pesticides are often sprayed onto fields to kill insects that damage and destroy crops. However, some of these chemicals can **pollute** the soil and make it more difficult for crops to grow in the future.

Pesticides are cheap and effective, but using them can harm the environment and ruin farming land. Pesticides are also damaging to humans and animals when they make their way into the food and water that we eat and drink. By paying farmers more for their crops, sustainable farming methods might solve problems like these.

Many people believe that fair trade rules will help the global economy. This is because all countries are linked by trade. Putting money into one country strengthens its economy, so the people living there can buy and sell more goods and services internationally. This helps strengthen the economies of other countries. As more and more countries strengthen their economies, the global economy will improve.

For example, by giving the vegetable farmers in a country more money for what they produce, more money is put into that country's economy. This helps the country's economy become stronger, because those farmers can afford to buy and sell more of what they produce. As the country's economy grows, it can take part in more international trade. The vegetable farmers can then also afford to produce more crops to sell internationally. All this trading helps make the global economy stronger.

It is easy to understand why fair trade is so important if we consider what happens when workers are exploited by businesses and other organizations that are looking for cheap goods and services, such as labor.

Businesses wanting to buy a certain crop, such as sugar cane, could buy it from a number of different farms in a number of different countries. With no fair trade rules in place, the business will try to buy the sugar cane for as little money as possible. The business can ask a farm to sell its sugar cane for a very low price. The farm doesn't have to agree, but the business might go to a different farm for cheaper sugar cane. That farm will lose the trade from that business, and perhaps others that are also looking for low prices. In this way, the farm is forced to sell its sugar cane for a low price.

BRAZIL GROWS TWICE AS MUCH SUGAR CANE AS ANY OTHER COUNTRY. MOST OF THIS SUGAR CANE IS USED TO MAKE SUGAR WHICH GETS EXPORTED TO OTHER COUNTRIES.

This plantation in Thailand is growing sugar cane. Sugar cane is one of the main plants that is used to make sugar.

If the sugar cane farm wasn't paid enough for its crops, it would need to look for other ways to make enough money to pay its workers and make a profit if possible. Profit is the money leftover when costs are paid. To make room to grow more crops, large areas of grassland or forest might be cleared. This would destroy **habitats**, but would mean the farm could make more money. Farms may also use pesticides that could damage the soil and harm habitats, but it would help the farm grow more sugar cane.

Often, farmers get paid so little that they cannot support their families, leaving them without proper homes or enough food to eat. Instead, the farmers may have to work long hours in dangerous conditions just to get enough money for food. If this isn't enough, the farm might start employing children at little to no money to work in the sugar cane fields. Businesses and organizations that set up factories in LEDCs also employ children for cheaper labor. Child labor is unfortunately very common in poor areas, where families need to make money to survive. Child labor and worker exploitation goes against **human rights**. Fair trade is one way that we can fight against worker exploitation and child labor.

ECONOMIES AROUND THE WORLD

STRONG ECONOMIES

There are many reasons why a country's economy might be strong. Some of the strongest national economies in the world are very different from one another—but they all usually have a range of goods, services, and resources that they export. For example, the United States has many companies that create the technology we use around the world. As technology is always in demand, this strengthens the country's economy. In Canada, many natural resources are exported to other countries, such as timber, oil, and metals mined from the ground.

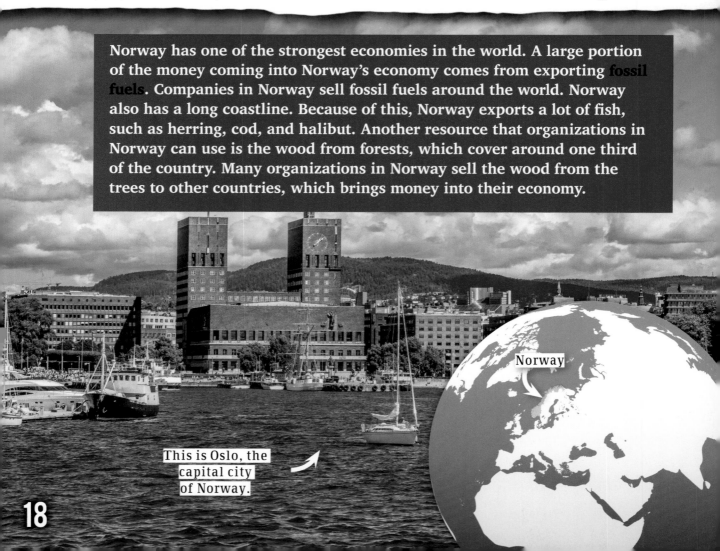

Norway has one of the strongest economies in the world. A large portion of the money coming into Norway's economy comes from exporting **fossil fuels**. Companies in Norway sell fossil fuels around the world. Norway also has a long coastline. Because of this, Norway exports a lot of fish, such as herring, cod, and halibut. Another resource that organizations in Norway can use is the wood from forests, which cover around one third of the country. Many organizations in Norway sell the wood from the trees to other countries, which brings money into their economy.

Norway

This is Oslo, the capital city of Norway.

While most countries with strong economies export many different goods, there are some countries that maintain a strong economy by exporting a large amount of only a few types of goods. One such country is Qatar, which is a tiny country in the Middle East. Despite being so small, Qatar exports more fossil fuels than almost any other country in the world. This brings a lot of money into the country's economy.

This is Doha, the capital city of Qatar.

Qatar

NATURAL GAS IS A TYPE OF FOSSIL FUEL AND IT IS FOUND DEEP UNDERGROUND. MORE NATURAL GAS IS MINED OUT OF THE GROUND IN QATAR THAN IN CHINA, A COUNTRY OVER 800 TIMES LARGER.

Qatar doesn't have a range of different resources that can be easily exported to other countries. While Norway, for example, has fossil fuels, wood, and fish that it can easily export, Qatar mostly exports fossil fuels. Exporting fossil fuels, such as oil and natural gas, makes up more than half of the money that comes into Qatar's economy. Almost everyone in the world uses fossil fuels, and prices are high, so Qatar is a very wealthy country. Its economy is strong and its citizens can afford to buy imported goods from all over the world.

WEAK ECONOMIES

Many factors can contribute to a weak economy. One common reason that contributes to a weak economy is a lack of resources in a country. Resources are often main exports for countries. Countries that do not have fossil fuels beneath the earth, **fertile** soil where crops can grow, water where people can catch fish, or forests where people can collect wood, often end up having a weak economy. For example, Burundi, in Africa, has one of the weakest economies in the world. It has few natural resources.

This is Bujumbura, the capital city of Burundi.

Burundi

Burundi is a landlocked country, which means that it does not have a coastline or access to the sea. This makes trading difficult for organizations in Burundi, because they do not have easy access to shipping methods. It also means that fishing cannot be done in the country. Burundi also does not have large forests and much of its soil is not suitable for farming. This is partly because the country is covered by mountains. Because of the lack of suitable cropland in Burundi, only a few crops such as coffee and tea are grown for export. Many people grow only the food they need to survive. With very few goods being exported from Burundi, little money comes into Burundi's economy from other countries.

Another country with a weak economy is Nepal. While Nepal faces many of the same problems as Burundi, such as being landlocked and having a lot of space taken up by mountains, many people believe that its economy struggles for other reasons.

Over the last 100 years, the government in Nepal has changed a lot. This has made it difficult for the country's economy to become stronger, which has affected the lives of the people who live in Nepal.

This is Kathmandu, the capital city of Nepal.

Nepal

Up until 1951, the king of Nepal kept the country **isolated** from the outside world. This meant that it did not trade with other countries and very few people from outside Nepal were allowed to enter the country. This stopped Nepal from keeping up with modern technology and left the country with poor schools, hospitals, and roads.

While the government in Nepal has made a lot of progress since 1951, the country's economy still struggles. Today, Nepali citizens who work in other countries send lots of money back home to their families. This money makes up a large portion of the money coming into Nepal's economy.

FAIR TRADE AND THE GLOBAL ECONOMY TODAY

THE GLOBAL ECONOMY

Today, every country in the world trades goods and services with other countries. They export goods and services to other countries to make money. They also import the goods and services that are used by their citizens. From the food we eat to the buses we take to school and the clothing we wear, we depend on international trade every day.

This map shows the main types of goods that are exported from each country.

- ■ Food/Drink
- ■ Metals/Materials
- ■ Wood Products
- ■ Oil
- ■ Textile/Apparel
- ■ Machinery/Transportation
- ■ Electronics
- ■ Other

Although it's not as easy to see, we rely on our country's exports as well as the imports that we use daily. The money a country makes from exporting goods usually improves the lives of its citizens. By exporting goods, a country brings money into its economy. In most cases, this helps strengthen the economy and allows the government to provide services, such as schools, hospitals, and parks, for its citizens. As every country's economy is affected by international trading and every person is affected by their country's economy, it is easy to see how the world truly does have a global economy. Every person is part of it and every person can be affected by it.

The global workforce is made up of all of the people who work to produce the goods and services that are traded between countries around the world. Fruit farmers in Brazil are part of the global workforce because their fruit gets exported. Miners, factory workers, and fishers are also part of the global workforce, because the goods they produce are exported to other countries.

People who are employed by organizations in other countries are part of the global workforce as well. In 1980, the global workforce was made up of around 1.2 billion people. Today, around 3 billion people—nearly half of the world's population—are part of the global workforce. Without international trading and the global economy, many of these jobs wouldn't exist.

All of these people are part of the global workforce.

We can see the huge impact of international trading when we look at the different foods available in our grocery stores. In typical North American grocery stores, people could buy tuna from South Korea, applesauce from Belgium, cherries from Chile, raspberries from Serbia, and bananas from Ecuador. Today, five different foods farmed in five different countries can all end up on the same shelf in a grocery store. By buying these foods, we are contributing to the global economy.

FAIR TRADE

As the global workforce has increased and countries have begun trading more goods and services with one another, fair trade has become even more important.

Today, there are many organizations that work to support fair trade and protect the human rights of the global workforce.

Fairtrade International is one of the largest fair trade organzations in the world. It is a non-profit organization, which means that the money it makes is used mostly to support the fair trade cause—instead of making money for itself. Fairtrade International evaluates different organizations that trade goods to see if their workers are getting a fair wage and are working in safe conditions. If the organization does not meet the Fairtrade Standards (see page 25), then Fairtrade International helps the workers receive more pay and safer working conditions.

THE FAIRTRADE STANDARDS

The Fairtrade Standards are a set of **criteria** that every trade organization should meet. The standards were made by Fairtrade International and they aim to help producers in the poorest countries in the world. Producers are the people who grow, mine, or make goods.

The Fairtrade Standards aim to:
- Make sure that producers are paid enough money to support themselves and cover costs of sustainable production methods
- Help producers have more control over who they trade with and establish trading partnerships
- Enhance the social, economic, and environmental development of communities
- Set clear criteria for production and trading of products.

Read more about Fairtrade International's standards at https://www.fairtrade.net/standards.html

While Fairtrade International does a lot to promote fair trade, it is not the only organization that does so. The World Fair Trade Organization helps make sure that businesses around the world follow their Ten Principles of Fair Trade, which are similar to the Fairtrade Standards. If a business shows the World Fair Trade Organization's logo (above), it means that they are committed to fair trade.

PROBLEMS WITH FAIR TRADE

Even though most people agree that fair trade is a good idea and could help a lot of people, there are some who believe that making people follow strict rules can actually stop their businesses and farms from doing well. For example, some people argue that sustainable farming is not realistic for poor farmers, as it is often more expensive than regular farming.

Fair trade organizations may find it difficult and dangerous to help producers in countries that are fighting a war.

In some countries, it is difficult for fair trade organizations to help producers of goods and services. Governments in some countries might not allow organizations that support fair trade to get involved there. Other times, citizens in countries experiencing conflict cannot produce sustainable goods because they may lose their land, money, or homes.

SUPPLY AND DEMAND

Supply and demand are important parts of the global economy. Supply is the amount of product that is available. Demand is the amount of people who want to buy the product. The supply of, and demand for, a product often determines how much money it is sold for. When demand is high, products can be sold for more money. But products are usually cheaper when there is more of them, because they are easier to buy. Imagine you are about to start selling lemonade on a beach on a hot day. Before you start selling, everyone on the beach is thirsty. When you start selling, everyone rushes up to buy the lemonade. As you are the only person selling lemonade, you can sell it at a high price.

Now imagine that five more people start selling lemonade on that same beach. Now, the supply is higher, and people can choose which person to buy lemonade from. If another person sells their lemonade for less money, people will choose to buy it from them, instead of you. This forces you to lower the price of your lemonade. Supply and demand is important in small economies, such as the beach, and in the global economy. Producers in many countries are forced to sell their products for lower prices, to keep customers. If fair trade products are much more expensive than other products, people may choose to buy the other products instead.

GET INVOLVED!

BUY FAIR TRADE

When you are shopping with your family, look for logos that show that a product has been fairly traded (see pages 24 and 25). You could see logos on products such as chocolate, coffee, bananas, flowers, and even footballs! These items may cost more money, but you will know that a fair amount of your money will go right to the producers.

SUPPORT THE CAUSE

Why not bake some cakes using fair trade ingredients, and have a cake sale to raise some money for an organization that supports fair trade? Or, you could make posters or an online **blog** to raise awareness about fair trade and its importance. Use the Internet to learn about producers of a certain product in a certain country, then raise awareness about their situation.

BECOME A FAIR TRADE SCHOOL

Did you know your school can become an official Fair Trade School? Organizations such as Fairtrade International and Fair Trade Campaigns can help your school support fair trade.

Schools can choose to purchase and use products that have been fairly traded. Your school can also teach you about fair trade, and help raise money and awareness for the cause. Ask your teacher about how your school can get involved.

If you are in the United States, learn more at http://fairtradecampaigns. org/campaign-type/schools/

If you are in Canada, learn more at http://fairtrade.ca/en-CA/Get-Involved/ Fair-Trade-Programs/Fair-Trade-Schools

SPREAD THE WORD

Talk to others about fair trade to help them learn about it and support the cause. Talk to your teacher about how to get involved. Find out more about where your food, clothing, and other items come from, and help people make good choices. Ask your parents to buy fair trade bananas. By sharing information, we can help make people's lives fairer and better.

ACTIVITY

 1 Design a fair trade snack for your school or grocery store! Research fair trade ingredients and think about the products mentioned in this book to create your snack.

 **2** What is the name of your snack?
What does the packaging look like?
What are the ingredients?
Don't forget the fair trade logo!

 3 What countries do your ingredients come from? If you don't know, how can you find out?

GLOSSARY

agriculture	Farming, growing crops, and raising animals to produce food and other products
blog	A website or web page where a person writes their thoughts regularly
citizens	The people who live in a certain country
clear-cutting	A logging technique in which all of the trees in an area are cut down
conditions	The state of something, such as an object or a person's surroundings
criteria	A set of standards by which something is judged
more economically developed countries	Countries with a strong economy, based on the amount of money made per person
less economically developed countries	Countries with a weaker economy, based on the amount of money made per person
equitable	Describing a solution that is fair, but sometimes different depending on the person and situation
Euro	The currency used by most members of the European Union, a partnership of countries in Europe including Germany and France
exploitation	The use of a person in a way that is unfair and unequal
fertile	Describing land that is very good for growing crops
fossil fuels	Fuels, such as coal, oil, and gas, that formed millions of years ago from the remains, or fossils, of animals and plants
goods	Resources that are transported between different countries
government	The group of people who control and make laws for a country
habitats	The natural homes of different animals and plants
human rights	Rights that every person should have, because they are human
isolated	Far away from animals, people or places
labor	Work; often hard physical work
natural resources	Materials such as trees, minerals, and water that occur naturally in a place
organizations	An organized group of people with a certain purpose, such as a business
pollute	Make poisonous or dirty by the actions of humans
ports	A town or city with access to water, where ships and boats can unload their goods
resources	Supplies of money, materials, food, or people that can be used to make money
transport	Move from one place to another using vehicles such as trucks, airplanes, and boats
services	A paid job which does not involve physical goods being exchanged
standard of living	The amount of money and comfort that a person has
sustainable	Able to be maintained; using only what is needed to keep environment balanced
wages	A regular payment for work

INDEX

A
agriculture 10–11
Asia 5, 11

B
bananas 11, 13, 21, 28–29
Burundi 20

C
Canada 7, 18, 29
child labor 17
citizens 4, 10, 12, 19, 20–22, 26
coffee 5, 11–12, 28
crops 10–11, 14, 16–17, 20

E
environment 13, 14, 25
exports 5, 7, 10, 12, 16, 18–19, 20, 22–23

F
farms, farmers 11, 13, 14–17, 21, 23, 25
food 10–11, 13, 14, 17, 18, 22–23, 29
forests 17, 18, 20
fossil fuels 18–19

G
global workforce 23, 24
goods 4–7, 9–13, 15, 16, 18–20, 22–26

I
imports 5, 7, 10, 19, 22, 24

J
jobs 10, 23

L
LEDCs 10–12, 17

N
Nepal 21
Norway 18

M
MEDCs 10–12
money 4, 7–11, 13, 15–22, 24–29

P
pesticides 14, 17
plantations 11, 16

Q
Qatar 19

R
resources 4–5, 7, 10, 18–20
rules 12, 15, 16, 26

S
services 4–6, 9, 10, 12–13, 15, 16, 18, 22–24, 26
sustainable farming 13, 14, 25, 26

T
technology 6–7, 18, 21
Thailand 10, 16

U
United States 5, 8–9, 18, 29

W
wage 13, 24